GW00832001

BAROTSELAND
and Scenes from Zambian Life

Tony Noel and Cedric Pulford

EDGE EDITIONS

www.ituri.co.uk

CONTENTS

PREFACE

The three articles gathered here depict Zambia and its
predecessor states at three historical stages: the advanced
Lozi (or Barotse) kingdom in what is now the Western
Province, the British period when the land was Northern
Rhodesia and post-independence Zambia.

The longest article, Tony Noel's Sunset over the Zambezi,
is a memoir of his time as a colonial official in the Fifties
and early Sixties. It shows us the hard work and loneliness
that such postings often entailed, as well as being a useful
reminder that the imperial experience was much more
nuanced than current simplifications and traducings
allow.

In News Media in Kaunda's Zambia and After, Cedric
Pulford records his more than two decades as a visiting
consultant. He saw the pressures on print, TV and radio in
a one-party state, and then the emergence of greater
(although not total) freedom of expression. The eternal
tussle between journalists and government is especially
acute in the Majority World. Journalists naturally want
what their peers in advanced countries enjoy while the
leaders of emerging economies and fragile states are
horrified by the negativity that often marks Western media
– the so-called 'Gotcha' style of journalism.

The first article is a historical overview of Barotseland. It
traces the evolution of this advanced African state –
famous for its Kuomboka river ceremony – through
successive land grabs by greedy speculators to absorption

into Northern Rhodesia and then reneging by the post-independence government of an autonomy agreement. A sad story indeed, which is regrettably not unique in Africa.

The three articles have been published before, although all may not be readily accessible. By bringing them together, it is hoped that these unassuming pieces will produce a Gestalt effect of the whole being greater than the sum of its parts – that is, giving a flavour of how Zambia became what it is today.

MH

BAROTSELAND: A UNIQUE AFRICAN KINGDOM
Historical overview by Cedric Pulford (2011)

It is one of Africa's most dramatic tourist attractions, but the water-borne Kuomboka ceremony of the Lozi people in western Zambia remains at the heart of their culture.

The Lozi were known in the days of the British Empire as the Barotse. These apparently different words are in fact one and the same, stemming from different conventions of registering sounds. Since this article is concerned about historical times, the older term Barotse is used here.

The Barotse occupy the flood plain of the River Zambezi up-river of the Victoria Falls in Zambia. The plain stretches for 120 miles and is 25 miles across at its widest. The annual flooding, between February and July, gave rise to a migratory, river culture whose symbol was the Kuomboka. The royal court led the move in the royal barge Nalikwanda to higher, drier ground at the plain edge, from the royal capital of Lealui to Limulunga. The Kuomboka is still re-enacted each year as the essence of Barotseland, now officially the Western Province of Zambia but once a proud and unique kingdom.

A detailed account of the river culture in traditional times was given by the anthropologist Max Gluckman in Economy of the Central Barotse Plain (1941). The Barotse typically spent three months at the plain margin because of flooding. On the plain itself high spots of land (mounds) were preferred for settlement because they rose above the water level. In later times, the margin became the most densely populated part of Barotseland.

All land was formally vested in the king, but his rights were limited in various ways. Pasturage was free; net fishing in deep waters, stabbing fish along the banks and killing birds and game were all permitted.

Before the British period (from the late 19th century), Barotse rule extended over an area larger than Germany, occupying 250,000 square miles at its largest. There were some 25 subject tribes. The administrative capital of Barotseland, now as in British times, is Mongu. The town lies on a bluff overlooking the Zambezi, a dramatic location chosen by the first British resident (official adviser) of the nation.

A curious historical interlude occurred in the mid-19th century when the Barotse were conquered by the Makololo, a branch of the Sotho from southern Africa. It was the Makololo overlords with their ruler Sebituane whom the missionary Dr David Livingstone encountered on his travels. Livingstone was much impressed by Sebituane, describing him in Missionary Travels and Researches in South Africa (1857) as 'decidedly the best th specimen of a native chief I ever met'. The king was fleet of foot and led warriors into battle himself. The explorer's historic journey to the African west coast was made with the help of the Makololo. In an illustration of the cheapness of human life (or alternatively of the value of firearms), Livingstone recorded that eight boys, the children of captive tribes, were exchanged for eight guns.

A further visit to Barotseland was described in Narrative of an Expedition to the Zambesi and Its Tributaries (1865), written with his brother, Charles. The Makololo, said the Livingstones, were 'by far' the most intelligent and enterprising of the tribes they had met – an observation that later observers were to apply the Barotse when they regained the ascendancy.

By now Sekeletu was the paramount chief. He and his subordinate chiefs expressed a wish for English settlers in the Batoka highlands, 'He said he would cut off a section of the country for the special use of the English; and on being told that in all probability their descendants would cause disturbance in his country, he replied, "These would be only domestic feuds, and of no importance".'

Although historically Barotseland had little in the way of a cattle culture, it is supposed to have been taught about cattle by the Makololo. An export trade to South Africa developed in the early British period. This was helped by the 1896 rinderpest epidemic in Southern Rhodesia. The trade did not proved lasting, however. It had largely disappeared by the First World War through bovine pleuro-pneumonia. The Makololo were eventually overthrown although they left behind the legacy of their language, which then became the tongue of the Barotse.

Lewanika the king

Out of this political upheaval emerged the man who was to become the most famous Litunga (king) of Barotseland, Lewanika. He wanted British protection from the nearby Matabele (originally from Zululand) under their leader

Lobengula, from the Portuguese and from some of his own dissident subjects.

Frank Lochner, representing Cecil Rhodes's Chartered Company, secured a far-reaching concession from Lewanika in 1890, the same year that the Company planted the flag in Lobengula's domains at what became Salisbury (now Harare). The concession covered all Lewanika's country, allowing the Company to engage in manufacturing, mining, banking, the provision of infrastructure works and the importation of arms and ammunition. Whatever Lewanika's fears of Lobengula, it is impossible to imagine that the Barotse king realised the full implications of such a one-sided deal. Within a few years his arch-rival was dead.

The 1893 Matabele war started over a small incident when the telegraph link was cut and wire stolen. The Chartered Company seized the opportunity and treated this as a casus belli. Maxim guns made short work of Lobengula's impis (regiments). The king fled his capital, Gubulawayo (close to today's Bulawayo), and soon died, probably of smallpox.

However, the process of assimilation was by now unstoppable for Lewanika. Barotseland became absorbed into Northern Rhodesia at first under the Company and, from 1924, as a British protectorate. The Lochner concession was followed by more treaties up to 1909. The Lawley concession of 1898 reduced Lewanika's annual subsidy from £2,000 to £850 and gave the Company judicial powers in disputes between whites or whites and blacks. It was the blueprint for the Lewanika concession of 1900. This affirmed the Company's administrative authority over the king's domains. It excluded prospecting in the Barotse heartland – and yet an astonishing postcript provided that if gold in worthwhile quantities was not found outside the reserved area, it could be sought inside the reserved area!

Col Colin Harding, who was a witness to the signatures on the treaty, wrote (Far Bugles, 1933) that 'on more mature consideration [Lewanika] realised that it carried him further than he had meant to go'. In a curious addition that may have been an attempt to distance himself from the deed, Harding went on:"'I would like to say here that although I was present when this Ratifying Treaty was signed and my name was appended as a witness to the other signatures, the full contents of the document were not divulged to me.'

There were more concessions to come. By a simple exchange of letters in 1904, Lewanika gave the Company farming and settlement rights throughout his kingdom except the Barotse valley and near Sesheke. The 1909 Wallace concession reiterated these farming and settlement rights except in areas where prospecting was prohibited (including the heartland). Villages and gardens were specifically allowed to be uprooted, albeit with consent and compensation. The consent need not be that of the people affected, however. It could also be given by the high commissioner of the territory – ie a Briton. This was a massive land grab, even if the worst of it never materialised by comparison with Southern Rhodesia. Nor were these deals made solely by rapacious commercial opportunists in Rhodes's name; they involved British imperial officials. It is hard now to understand how these people could bless such unequal treaties. It is equally hard to imagine why Lewanika and his advisers gave away so much.

Two points may be made in support of Lewanika, who remains a hero to the Lozi. He kept the Barotse heartland intact and the British came to his country by treaty, not conquest. Thus Barotseland differed from Lobengula's kingdom, and merited different treatment in Lozi eyes and also to a degree in those of colonial officials. The situation may be compared with what is now Uganda. There, Buganda reached an accommodation with the incoming British and for ever after was treated better than the rival kingdom of Bunyoro, which had to be subdued by force of arms (see Cedric Pulford, Eating Uganda, 1999, Casualty of Empire, 2007, and Two Kingdoms of Uganda, 2011).

In Barotseland as in much of the empire, the British style was to rule without overt displays of power. Norman Knight recounts how as a young district officer he was borne home in state by bearers, to the anger of the provincial commissioner, who happened to see the incident. There was a good reason – Knight had been injured – but he had some explaining to do (Memories of a District Officer in Northern Rhodesia and of the War Years, 2007).

Meanwhile, the indifference of colonialism to traditional boundaries was illustrated by the King of Italy's boundary award of 1905. This sliced a huge chunk from Lewanika's domains, allocating it to Portugal. Catherine Winkworth Mackintosh claimed (Coillard of the Zambesi, 1907) that the king was probably left with as much as he had ever occupied effectively. He lost more than a quarter of his land but still had 181,947 square miles, not greatly short of Germany's 208,947 square miles. Another loss of territory occurred in 1941 when, within Northern Rhodesia, Balovale district, where the Lozi had long claimed overlordship, was excised from Barotseland.

Colin Harding, who travelled up the Zambezi from Victoria Falls to Lealui, gave an account (In Remotest Barotseland, 1905) of Lewanika's daily routine. He sat in the courthouse between 9am and 10am, hearing complaints, promulgating laws and attending to other government business. The indunas, or senior officials, representing the people, sat on his right. They alone had the right to criticise the king. In Far Bugles, Harding praised Lewanika's 'charming personality', his 'loyalty and other inherent virtues'. When the Litunga visited London for the coronation of King Edward VII, with Harding in attendance, the king and his retinue were found not to touch alcohol. 'Lewanika's whole and consistent attitude was befitting a gentleman and a great native ruler,' Harding wrote.

More than sixty years later Lewanika was still winning praise. A 1968 biography by Gervas Clay, Your Friend, Lewanika, could not speak too highly of the Litunga. 'He died full of honour, loved and respected by his people as a great chief, leaving the heart of his country reserved to the Barotse by treaty rights and his own family secure on the throne. No African ruler of his time achieved more, and none was more regretted by all who had known him.'

Independence and after

Barotseland enjoyed a large degree of autonomy under the British. However, this once leading state, afflicted by its remoteness, slipped into backwardness. Development in

Northern Rhodesia became focused on the mining areas and along the line of rail from Livingstone through Lusaka to the Copperbelt. In recent times, as Gerald L. Caplan points out in The Elites of Barotseland 1878-1969 (1970), the country has been an underpopulated labour reserve with 1/6th of the land mass but less than 1/10th of the population of Zambia.

Barotse autonomy was at first maintained when the colony became Zambia in 1964. Later, it was removed, leading to long-running resentments at least among the elites. The special status of Barotseland had been reaffirmed pre-independence by the Monckton Commission in 1960. But the United National Independence Party (UNIP) of Kenneth Kaunda beat Barotse secessionists in elections at various levels in 1962, 1963 and 1964. Kaunda and the Litunga signed the Barotseland Agreement in 1964, independence year, but Zambia's new leader evidently felt under no obligation to respect it. The following year the Local Government Act abolished the Litunga's independent powers and the Barotse National Council was replaced by five district councils.

By now the Barotse electorate were awakening to what they had signed up for. In the 1968 national elections, UNIP lost eight of the province's 11 constituencies. But it was too late. The Litunga lost his control of land, which was transferred to the state. The Barotseland Agreement was abolished in 1969, leaving all eight Zambian provinces on an equal footing for the first time but also leaving a legacy of bitterness among the Barotse that continues to this day. Barotseland now became the Western Province.

Coillard the missionary

Although David Livingstone 'discovered' Barotseland, Francois Coillard was the missionary who exerted the greatest influence in the early years of European contact. Lewanika said: 'There are three sorts of whites, those of the government, the traders and missionaries. Fear those of the government, they have power; prey on the traders, for they have come to prey on you. As for the missionaries, a missionary is one of us.' (Quoted by Clay, above.)

Coillard (1834-1904), a French Protestant of the Paris Evangelical Mission, stayed in the country for many years and was close to Lewanika. On the Threshold of Central Africa (1897, from the original in French) is his account of the experience.
The missionary had worked for twenty years among the Sotho in Basutoland (now Lesotho). When he came north his first plan was to work among the Banyai, who were under the Matabele. But Lobengula said no, and Coillard went to Barotseland instead. At that point, 1877, the Makololo (who were Sotho) had not long been overthrown. They had treated the Barotse well, hence Coillard and his fellow envangelists were accepted by the Litunga and much of the country.

Coillard settled in Barotseland in 1880, remaining there (apart from two years' leave in Europe in the late-Nineties) until his death in 1904, aged sixty-nine. His dominance in the mission field was threatened for a time by a movement known as the Ethiopian church. It flickered out relatively soon but remained a beacon for the later emergence of indigenous African associations.

The French missionary instinctively favoured the Chartered Company as the agent of 'civilising' European influence. 'Coillard ... gave Lochner (see above) all the support he could. Coillard viewed with distrust the whole structure of the Barotse state as it was imbued with paganism,' Lewis Gann writes in The Birth of a Plural Society (1958). Barotse chiefs vetoed Lewanika's conversion to Christianity for political reasons, although his son and successor, Letia, was a Christian. The king read his bible almost daily but was said (by Catherine Mackintosh in Lewanika of the Barotse, 1942) also to sacrifice to his ancestors. 'Read' is apparently not to be understood literally. A European pioneer, R.H. Palmer (Reminscences of a Pioneer, undated), reported that Lewanika could not read or write Sekololo, nor could he speak English. Palmer added that Lewanika was nevertheless a natural ruler. This sentiment is widely shared, as we saw above.

Barotse way of life

The Barotse's elite status vis a vis subject tribes was underlined by the 1911 edition of the Enclyclopaedia Britannica, which described them as 'the intellectual and physical superiors of the vast majority of the negro races of Africa'. Barotseland in pre-colonial times had the economic characteristics of a state reaching beyond local or tribal groups. Gann, in The Birth of a Plural Society, says the country had some regional economic specialisation with the different parts interdependent.
The constitutional arrangements were unusual, the Litunga reigning jointly with a queen, the Mokwai, who was his eldest sister. The Mokwai had a separate capital, Nalolo, to the south of Lealui. Barotseland's religio-social

arrangements were also curious, at least to European eyes. V.W. Turner (The Lozi Peoples of North-Western Rhodesia, 1952) describes a religion in which the supreme god was not omnipotent. His name was Nyambe, and his wife was Nasilele. He was driven n from earth into heaven by man.

D.W. Stirke, who spent eight years among the Barotse and whose book proclaimed exactly that (Eight Years Among the Barotse, 1922), claimed that children of similar ages started sexual relations almost as soon as they could walk. The not surprising result was that virginity was unknown. The Mwalianzo ceremony marked a girl's first menstruation, after which she was married. There was no offence of rape. On the other hand, according to Stirke, there was no known case of a girl needing coercion – a conclusion that feminists today would certainly challenge.

Catherine Mackintosh, who was the niece of Francois Coillard, quoted her uncle (in Coillard of the Zambesi) on the impermanence of marriage among the Barotse. This was because of the ease of divorce. 'There are no unhappy couples here; they part,' said Coillard.

In 1906, under British encouragement, Lewanika proclaimed the abolition of slavery in his kingdom. He had been struck on a visit to England by the sight of people working for themselves. Everybody seemed to be at work, but in his country 'people just sit about'. Abolition must have caused much disruption in the kingdom. Both Catherine Mackintosh and a visitor, Reginald Arthur Luck, spoke of widespread slavery. Luck said (A Visit to Lewanika, King of the Barotse, 1902): 'Slave trading is supposed to be at an end, but as a matter of fact, all the surrounding tribes are slaves to the Barotse.'

Mackintosh, in Lewanika of the Barotse, said that apart from the Barotse, no-one else was free in the country; the rest were slaves. Max Gluckman said the Barotse fought to gain women and children as servants, not men as warriors. In this they contrasted with the Zulu and their kinfolk, the Ndebele. Neither the subordinate tribes nor the Barotse themselves regret the passing of the old order, said Gluckman, writing in the 1940s. 'Almost all' Barotse consider modern times better than the old. He was writing in the late colonial period, and found an absence of white-Barotse tensions. With post-colonial hindsight, we may wonder whether this was colour (and economic) blindness or merely an acceptance of the inevitable.

Hindsight too has its limitations. Twilight on the Zambesi by Eugenia W. Herbert (2002) is one of the few recent books to touch on Barotseland. She cautions us to 'resist the temptation simply to see "colonialism" and "nationalism" as so many abstractions ... [it is] much easier to divide the actors willy-nilly into good guys and bad guys and move on. Everyone acknowledges that their own lives are a lot more complicated than that, but we often fail to grant the same complexity to the past.' She points out that the Zambian government has behaved just as stingily towards Barotseland as the colonial treasury.

It was Barotseland's misfortune to be caught up in wider imperial politics in one of its most sensitive areas, southern Africa. Cecil Rhodes dreamt of an 'all red' route from the Cape to Cairo. Gladstone's administration, according to John Marlowe's Cecil Rhodes: The Anatomy of

Empire (1972), went along with Rhodes's Chartered Company, preferring its 'unscrupulous and insubordinate methods' to the weakness of the counterpart company in east Africa. Rhodes's dream of all-red territory the length of Africa materialised in 1918, long after his death, when Britain obtained the United Nations mandate over the former German colony of Tanganyika. However, the 'iron spine', a railway, to connect all the territory, was never built.

A BAROTSELAND BIBLIOGRAPHY

Caplan, Gerald L. The Elites of Barotseland 1878-1969. (C. Hurst & Co, 1970)
Clay, Gervas. Your Friend, Lewanika (Chatto & Windus, 1968)
Coillard, Francois. On the Threshold of Central Africa. (First published 1897. Original in French. Republished by Frank Cass & Co, 1971)
Flint, Lawrence S. Historical Constructions of Postcolonial Citizenship and Subjectivity: the Case of the Lozi Peoples of Southern Central Africa (unpublished PhD thesis, University of Birmingham, 2006)
Gann. L.H. The Birth of a Plural Society (Manchester University Press, 1958)
Gluckman, Max. Economy of the Central Barotse Plain (Rhodes-Livingstone Institute, Livingstone, 1941)
Grotpeter, John J, Siegel, Brian V and Pletcher, James R. Historical Dictionary of Zambia (Scarecrow Press, 1998)
Harding, Lt Col Colin. Far Bugles (Simpkin Marshall, 1933)
Harding, Col Colin. In Remotest Barotseland (Hurst & Blackett, 1905)

Herbert, Eugenia W. Twilight on the Zambesi (Palgrave Macmillan, 2002)

Knight, Norman. Memories of a District Officer in Northern Rhodesia and of the War Years (privately published, 2007)

Livingstone, David. Missionary Travels and Researches in South Africa (Ward, Lock & Co, 1857)

Livingstone, David and Charles. Narrative of an Expedition to the Zambesi and Its Tributaries (John Murray, 1865)

Luck, Reginald Arthur. A Visit to Lewanika, King of the Barotse (Simpkin, Marshall, Hamilton, Kent & Co, 1902)

Mackintosh, C.W. Coillard of the Zambesi (T. Fisher Unwin, 1907)

Mackintosh, C.W. Lewanika of the Barotse (United Society for Christian Literature, 1942)

Marlowe, John. Cecil Rhodes: The Anatomy of Empire (Paul Elek, 1972)

Palmer, R.H. Lewanika's Country: Reminiscences of a Pioneer (privately printed, undated)

Stirke, D.W. Barotseland: Eight Years Among the Barotse (John Bales, Sons & Daniellson, 1922)

Turner, V.W. The Lozi Peoples of North-Western Rhodesia (International African Institute, London, 1952)

SUNSET OVER THE ZAMBEZI
Memories of Northern Rhodesia: 1958 - 1965

By TONY NOEL

FIRST TOUR   **Eastern Province Katete**   **Chadiza**

In January 1958 I embarked on the Union Castle liner Durban Castle berthed in George V docks, London. We sailed to Rotterdam then down the Channel with a force nine easterly gale behind us to push us out into the Atlantic. On day three the thrill of being driven forward by such an elemental force was replaced by warm sunshine, late in the evening we docked at Las Palmas, and walked along the quay under the palms enjoying the soft air. Then we steamed south, crossing the equator for the first time I, among many who had never crossed the Line, was properly inducted by King Neptune, lots of shaving soap then into the pool. The next call was Ascension Island no landing permitted and then St Helena where we anchored off shore but went up the wooded mountain in an old bus to see Napoleon's residence where he was in exile. During the voyage I celebrated my 21st and with a group of friends who I had met, we enjoyed a splendid party on deck until at midnight the stern Master at Arms sent us off to our cabins, discipline even for passengers was still strict in those days! Although leaning on the rail with a companion looking at the phosphorescence in our wake reflecting in the moonlight was permitted. Finally early one morning Table Mountain appeared on the horizon. Cape Town remains one of the most beautiful cities in the world, and to approach at dawn after eighteen days at sea is a vision that cannot be surpassed. The light climbs over Table

Mountain and illuminates the buildings and the bay in shades of gold.

After we had docked several of us travelling north went to a hotel for two nights to await the weekly train to Lusaka. Next morning I went up Table Mountain on the cable car for the first time, a wonderful experience. Then next day to the station to catch the train north, it left just after lunch and slowly steamed through the wine lands and mountains of the Cape, next morning we were in the desert of the Karoo, seemingly endless empty scrub. The line runs through Botswana, then Bechuanaland, stopping frequently for water when the train was surrounded by women and children selling curios and fruit. It took three days to reach Bulawayo in the evening, where those going to Salisbury had to change, we went on through the night and crossed the Zambezi over the Victoria Falls in the morning, and very late that evening we finally reached Lusaka, four days later and 2,000 miles north!

After a day for some briefing, this was the first time I had been told my destination, and shopping for essential kit. I was driven by Landrover the 400+ miles up the Great Eastern Road to Katete, gravel all the way, with an overnight stop at a government rest house in the hills above the Luangwa River. At Katete I met my district commissioner Tony Andrews, and his wife June. His father had been DC Nazareth in the thirties and was murdered by the Irgun, he features in Hugh Foot's, Lord Caradon, autobiography as a mentor to Hugh when he was a young cadet in Palestine. Tony was certainly also a great teacher; my first challenge was to learn the local language, Chinyanja, so after about four weeks when I was sent out on tour for aweek, the messengers were all suddenly unable to speak English, I am sure they had done so at the Boma, as the government office was called. I was sent to a remote backward area of little importance on the edge of the Luangwua escarpment, hilly, poor soil and very small villages. The only significance I recall was viewing the remains of an ancient car which the chief had bought many years earlier, it was alleged it never ran but was pulled by oxen. After any tour a report was expected on the area visited, potential issues, development possibilities and so forth, goodness knows what I submitted but it must have been acceptable. The role of the District Messenger was critical to the running of the administration. He was both the local policeman with powers of arrest, the DC's eyes and ears, and like the NCOs in the army was used to break in new young DO's. On tour I was totally reliant on him as guide and mentor. Most had experience in the military some of ours having served in Burma.

Katete was designated as a development district, there were about 10 to15 European staff on the station, a DC, 2 district officers plus agricultural and other development staff in including the teaching staff for a trades school, the headmaster was from Northern Ireland, by attitude and demeanour surely a cousin of Ian Paisley, although he had not come to public notice then. Most of the married staff had three or four bedroom bungalows; I was allocated a prefabricated house called a terrapin, set on stilts, which wobbled when you stepped in, small but quite adequate for a bachelor. We had no electricity, just Tilley lamps a wood stove, and a 'Rhodesian boiler' for hot water; that was two forty-four gallon drums built above a fire place and piped into the house. Cookie would light the fire early in the morning, all mod cons in central Africa! If I had a fridge it would have been run on paraffin.

Volcanic out crops, kopjes in local parlance, were a major feature in the Eastern Province and Katete District was dominated by this magnificent mount, Chipili Hill, a northern extension of the range that runs along the eastern edge of Africa. It was on the border with Mozambique, I never had the chance to climb it but it was widely believed to have sacred significance to the local Chewa people. The area was quite densely populated and cultivated. Across the border it was very sparsely populated, The old men told me that was because of the manner of Portuguese rule.

The next few months were spent on a variety of mainly practical tasks, supervising the building of a new prison, clearing roads and building drifts, a local term for a ford with a level concrete base. One enjoyable project was running the Katete Show, an annual event to highlight progress and sell development messages. Great fun as some ten thousand villagers came for the day, all chewing sugar cane as a snack; the residue spat out was a deep mulch across the ground. One innovation I created, at the instigation of one of the messengers, Ayenella, was to build a snake pit. He caught the snakes I just supervised the construction. He belonged to a special sect the Vinyau, with knowledge of herbs and potions which he used to calm the snakes. The week before the show there was much excitement when he came in with a black mamba. I have never seen anything so evil looking; fortunately it died as he said he had given it too much 'mutti', medicine. I was much relieved as the prospect of such a dangerous creature was quite frightening.

It was shortly after the show, probably at Ayenella's instigation that we had an invitation to witness a dance ceremony in one of the villages. We arrived after dark and could hear the drumming as soon as we got out of the Landrover. It was a Vinyau dance, we sat on logs around a cleared area and soon the masked dancers started, soon men and women joined in and the hypnotic rhythms began to dominate. They were very powerful, it was alleged that any adultery claim at such an event would not be substantiated under customary law, understandable in the atmosphere that evening. By the time we left a goodly number were dancing with great energy and enthusiasm, you got the impression it might go on all night. The more common dance locally was the Chimtali, positively tame in comparison.

By October the temperature had climbed well into the thirties, rain was due usually in November and it steadily grew hotter and more humid. One lunch time I was sitting in my terrapin when I was summoned to the prison building site; I was in charge of the project which involved making several thousand bricks, we had finished the dormitory blocks and were starting on the external wall. All the prisoners had been taken ill!

There was a mission hospital about four miles away so I drove there to see the prisoner builders sitting in the shade of a tree, looking rather green and vomiting frequently. The mission doctor stood nearby with a text book in hand; *'The first time I have ever seen such clear evidence of arsenical poisoning'*, was his comment. My plea was for action, but he assured me nature would take its course, which of course it did. The footings for the prison wall had been treated with sulphate of arsenic to deter

white ants, and the builders had drunk from the same
bucket without bothering to rinse it first! The significance
of the event was twofold; firstly this happened a few weeks
after the publicity about 'atrocities' at the Hola Mau Mau
detention camp in Kenya, and secondly this was the first
time I had been in charge of the station for the day so my
career could have been ended there and then!

Much of the work of the station was the supervision of the
local Native Authority, run by the chiefs and elders; our
job was to audit the accounts on a regular basis. Very
boring, sitting in a smelly mud built office checking
receipts for licences, which frequently did not add up.
These discussions became easier as my knowledge of the
language improved and I passed my exams, basic and
higher. Other tours of the villages followed, as Katete was
a development station we had several areas where farmers
were following guidance from the Agricultural specialists in
improved techniques, manuring, crop rotation and so
forth, grain prices were high at the time and were making
a good living.

We had a local co-op which bought the produce for
shipment down to Lusaka, the manager was Peter Matoka
, good company with his wife Grace, many years later he
was appointed Zambian High Commissioner in London.
Two of us used to visit them of an evening to play chess
and cards and they made us most welcome, although they
were not socially accepted by most of the European staff.

Katete was only forty miles from the Luangua Valley and I
enjoyed several weekend trips down to the game reserves,
staying in the game camps and walking with the rangers to
view game quite scary when you walk up to a rhino hiding

under a tree.On one occasion I went down with our local
road foreman Jani Scheepers, a typical Afrikaner but close
to the land, We slept in the open near the river and caught
a very large catfish, perhaps 50lbs; after landing it was
tethered by a wire through its gills; it just lay in the water,
in the evening as it cooled the fish made a jerk, sapped the
steel trace and was away. By this time Tony Andrews had
left on leave and a new DC called Beck had taken over. He
was a strange guy, drove an ancient Rolls Royce, was very
intense and could not understand why I enjoyed a beer
with Jani, who was considered to be reactionary and a bad
South African influence.

Jani did have the last word however; he woke me up at
6am, one morning, his greeting was 'Hey man the natives
are marching on the Boma, you must get up. (not his
precise words I might say). So I drove out about five miles
down the Great East Road and came upon a group of
African men walking along towards the Boma with guns on
their shoulders. What Jani had failed to tell me was one of
our District Messengers brought up the rear, he had
arrested them for failing to pay their gun licences. We piled
the muzzle loaders into the back of the vanette and shortly
the men came into the Boma to pay their dues. A typical
days work for one of our district messengers.

How sad that that story could never be repeated in today's
Africa where AK47s are more prevalent than muzzle
loaders. In retrospect these two stories of Jani and the
Matokas illustrate how conflicted race relations were. The
consensus was that I was starting a long career; my
experience of Ghanaian independence was dismissed as
irrelevant!

One particular aspect of Katete was the residue of a farming community established many years earlier in the days before the building of the railway when Fort Jamieson, now Chipapa, was the gateway to the territory.

The most interesting character was a formidable lady called Mrs Jerominsky, whose farm grew the most delicious oranges I have ever tasted. The farm was started by her husband before the First World War; he combined elephant hunting in the dry season and farming in the rains. The story goes that he pined for a wife, so after the war consulted a catalogue, marked his preferred choice and then walked down to Dar es Salaam to meet the boat. There was a mix up, but he married the girl who had come and they walked back to the farm, about 500+ miles. By now most of the dry season had passed so she was left alone to run the farm while he went down the Luangua for his elephants. She survived long after he had died and entertained us with her fabulous oranges in her Victorian parlour. She always wore a cotton dress, a heavy leather belt with an enormous bunch of keys, and surrounded by a pack of mangy dogs, mostly wounded by leopards that lived in the hills, or by baboons that raided the farm. She ran the farm alone with her son and when later the farms were taken over by the government moved down to Southern Province. There were one or two other farmers in the district, one kindly wife, a Mrs Van Wyck, gave me a lift to Lusaka, when I had a short break. As we sped across a wide dambo, maybe a mile across, she said 'crossing that dambo took four days when she journeyed up for the first time in the1920s. Then it was well maintained gravel road; now tarmac all the way.

I spent two weekends at Lundazi where the Castle Hotel
served as the Government Rest House; a splendid building
with service and cuisine to match, built in the depression
of 1931-32 in the style of a medieval castle by a DC as a
work project to inject cash into the local economy,
allegedly using his own funds. A beautiful area and my
preferred next posting; however I went to Chadiza instead.
This was a tiny station on the Nyasaland border, now
Malawi. This was a very poor district away from the main
Great East Road. The DC was Bill Oliver, a delightful
protestant Irishman, great company with equal capacity
for the booze. We were only three European families and
me, but it was quite an enjoyable posting. The duties were
the same as at Katete, touring and a mix on office work
and limited development, I do remember we were putting a
water supply into a primary school, had built a water
tower and were installing the supply, a three inch pipe.
The day I visited the children had managed to snap this
pipe; I was furious and suggested they all be punished, he
was more tolerant and put it down to high spirits.
One visit by the Rhodesian army turned out to be fun;
firstly they did a fly past with a Canberra bomber at low
level, designed by the Federal Government to impress the
local population, it certainly terrified me. Then the army
platoon challenged me and my district messengers to take
them on a night exercise. Many of the messengers were
former askaris who had served in the Burma Campaign. I
guess we did not play fair when we slipped over a hill
attacked from the rear, undefended, disabling the army
vehicles 'borrowing their rotor arms'! I gathered they were
not amused by being out witted by a national service
lieutenant. This was my last day in Chadiza so they took
revenge and emptied my drinks cupboard before leaving.

I remember well Christmas there, spent mainly in the pool of a local agriculture station. Quite a crowd had come in including a White Father, a member of a Catholic order focused on Africa who did not take a vow of poverty. He was enjoying himself with us until about 4pm when he looked at his watch and said he must be off; he was riding his small motorbike about fifty miles down into the Luangwa Valley to a small village where he was expected to take communion, he had no kit or food, and would be dependent on the village. His ability to move from the affluence of our European society to level with the African villagers still amazes me today; it is a rare gift.

The provincial headquarters was Fort Jameson, now Chipapa, fifty miles away. This little town had a long history as it was in many ways the foundation of Northern Rhodesia. The early pioneers came through Nyasaland then walked across the Luangwa valley to open up the Copper Belt long before the railway from the south was built. The airport was there, serviced by elderly Dakotas; as I sat awaiting take-off, a chap wearing a gabardine raincoat sitting in an aisle seat suddenly got up walked to the front saying, 'Well if no one else is going to do it I had better take this old crate back to Lusaka', and off we flew.

I was summoned to Fort Jameson for two events; a visit by the Monkton Commission which was to decide on the future of the Federation was the most memorable. The African population in Northern Rhodesia and Nyasaland had always opposed the Federation, hence the display of military might I described earlier. I was told to man the bar for an evening reception for the noble Lord Monckton. No problem as I set out the drinks and glasses, until as I picked up an ice bucket, my hand touched the cold glass, a loud explosion followed; a policeman carrying a machine gun jumped through the window, the DC arrived in his braces, all very exciting not like our quiet bush life.

Later I was called to help with the Queen Mothers visit but that was for me low key, I cannot even remember what I had to do.

Whilst at Chadiza I was sent to the government training centre outside Lusaka for a development course, I must have done all right because I was then put forward for promotion to District Officer at the end of my first three year tour. It was early in 1960 that I flew home for my first leave; from Lusaka to Brazzaville, then Kano in Nigeria, where I spent a week with Jack Aspden in Kaduna where the regiment was based, then Kano, Rome London, where we disembarked into the line of prefabs, temporary buildings as the airport terminals had yet to be built. After a few days back at Orchards I travelled to Germany, picked up a new VW from the factory at Wolfsburg, I remember it cost £299!

The first trip was north to Hamburg where the Coles family were living, after a few days there the car went in for its first service, a most impressive affair, a line of about eight bays, in the first a team of white coated technicians marched in taking parts off, into the second repeat performance and so on until the last bay when the foreman took my precious car and drove round the park at outrageous speed, back into another bay for further attention, when finally it was declared acceptable. After Hamburg I drove south to Austria, Innsbruck then Vienna for some fabulous Mozart, returning to UK after a lengthy stay on the continent and over a thousand miles in the car.

SECOND TOUR   Bancroft   Solwezi   Lusaka

It was late in 1960 when I went back to Northern Rhodesia for my second tour. This time I sailed from Southampton on a mail boat, so only a two week journey, not the magic of that first sea voyage. I had to go Southampton early for my new VW to be loaded and I had also bought a hunting rifle which had been delivered directly to the boat. The mail boats sailed directly to Cape Town. No leisurely stops as on the first trip.

Arrival at Cape Town was quite hilarious, the rifle which I had not seen was in a wooden crate, this had to be opened, and then the customs officer started to march the porters up and the down the baggage hall at the point of the rifle which he lovingly caressed. Bearing in mind there were several hundred passengers waiting to clear customs, this was not widely appreciated. 'You will need this up there lad' was the comment. Such was South African humour in the Sixties!

The crate was stowed in the VW once it was off loaded and I started the long, four days, 2,500 miles drive, north to Bancroft on the Copperbelt, where I was welcomed by the DC and his wife, Roy and Ishbell Stokes. Roy had many years of experience as a DC having come out to NR in 1940 on an armed merchant ship which docked at Lobito Bay, and thence by train through Angola. This line was destroyed in the civil wars in the 1970s and has never reopened. He told the story of how he was trained to man the one gun mounted on the prow and had to stand watch, on one occasion opening fire on a 'submarine' surfacing near the vessel; it was a whale, and he missed!

Before settling in to Bancroft, now a fledgling District Officer, I was summoned to meet the Senior Provincial Commissioner, James Murray at Ndola. Politically it was a sensitive time; Roy Welensky was talking about independence for Southern Rhodesia, there were rumours about the RAF assembling in Kenya, and many Europeans in the community and on the mines had sympathies with Rhodesia / South Africa, so I was quizzed about my loyalties to the Crown. I had to explain that as an army officer they should not be in doubt, this convinced Mr Murray.

Bancroft was the smallest of the mining towns, with a European population of over 2,000; it had all the mod cons of modern living, running water, electricity, and a thriving town centre with shops, chemist, banks and so forth. The United Reformed Church of NR, run by a Canadian Minister, Eric Read was close by. This was my first experience of urban life in Africa; the mines were vital to the country's economy and our prime role was to ensure the economy prospered. It was very different to life as a DO in the bush; mostly paperwork, with limited visits to the mine township where the African workers lived. Shortly after arriving at Bancroft, it was the long Easter weekend, I drove the seven hundred miles back to Katete to collect my dog Spooks, a little black mongrel.

A few weeks later we had a new labour officer appointed to join our team. Richard McVean, he was a great social asset, not only for his company but also because he had a bright red Sunbeam Alpine, open top two seater, which we

enjoyed on the smooth tarmac roads of the Copperbelt
,travelling to the sophisticated night club in Kitwe, a
different world for me but great fun while it lasted. After a
few months Richard was called to take part in an inquiry
into working conditions on the mines, and was then
headhunted to join Anglo American, the mining company
in Salisbury. We were all naturally very envious. Salisbury
was seen as the epitome of civilised living! However
unknown to me at the time Richard was in the future to
play a major role in my life.

The mining company housing was on a small hill with the
general manager's house on top with the other manager's
houses descending in rank order. One evening the DC was
invited to drinks and I was in his party. The reception was
held in the manager's lounge, the floor was tiled in green
malachite, stunningly beautiful, with a view to match. The
mine had a hospital run by Dr Namalonga, if I remember
his name correctly. He was from Barotseland, had been
trained in Durban and spoke with great fondness of his
time there as a student. None of the usual horror stories of
the South African police but typical relations between
medics and police. I was a frequent visitor to his house,
where his wife and family made me most welcome. Another
experience in Bancroft was a trip down the mine. The
major problem was excess water, the mine had been closed
previously and if the pumps stopped the mine would flood
again. So having been kitted out down I went down with
one of the staff. It was not pleasant, hot, wading through
water a foot deep. I was pleased to come up after a few
hours, even more pleased never to have to repeat the
experience.

Another social attraction was the theatre in Chingola, a much larger mining town a few miles away which had a theatre. Not only did they mount high standard amateur productions but they hosted visiting touring companies. One, from South Africa was Ipi Tombi, an exciting production of sophisticated African dancing, great fun, it was later developed and moved to London where it had a good run.

Bancroft had another local disused mine, Konkolla, which I believe has since been reopened; it was a bit spooky like an old Cornish tine mine. . A few miles further on was the Congo border, the great exodus of Belgians had been the previous year but there was little activity at that time. Then a rumour began of a new African exodus, so off I was sent in our little vanette with a couple of messengers to establish the facts. We picked up the Congolese border guard and drove on a few miles before we were stopped by a rifle toting guy wearing military gear, I noticed both my messengers were as white as me, it was a new experience to have a rifle pointed at you! The border guard was in the back, his protestations highly voluble; but all was well although we failed to find any evidence of potential refugees.

At Bancroft there was no court work. It was handled by visiting magistrates, but to prepare me for my next posting I was sent to Ndola for a week to train with a senior magistrate. I had to sit with him as the evidence was heard, and then write a judgement on what was presented. He would then read this, comment and allow me to read his own findings. It reminded me of lessons at school on writing precis. At this time there was a United Nations Inquiry into the Dag Hammarskjold air crash; he was the

UN Secretary General involved in a peace process during the first Congo war, when his plane crashed whilst trying to land at Ndola airport. There had been much rumour and even today controversy remains over the cause but the final conclusion was conveniently recorded as pilot error.

After a year in Bancroft I was posted out to the North Western Province to Solwezi, the provincial headquarters, a total change of environment. Our district offices adjoined those of the Provincial Commissioner, a fierce ex Indian Army officer with a tendency to raise his voice; however, he was well matched by his secretary, a former army wife well versed in such matters with a controlled deafness when necessary.

Solwezi was 100 miles northwest of the Copperbelt on a reasonable gravel road, laterite was the local term, but difficult in the rains. The district bordered the Congo for many miles. There was a substantial European population, a police station and a few traders, but none of the urban facilities as in Bancroft.

My main memory of touring in Solwezi was of visiting the part of the district that covered the Kafue headwaters. The Kafue was the most important river in NR providing water to both the Copperbelt, and then downstream to Lusaka. Most villages had been moved out of the area years before, but we had to patrol to ensure no significant area of cultivation had been cleared, which would result in silting and contamination of the river. An early ecological project before the term had been invented! My memories of those tours were of mud, rain, cold nights in camp, and humping my bicycle through muddy dambos, marshy stream beds, favoured for dry season cultivation, but very damaging from an environmental point of view.

The word touring has implications of a gentle progression; this picture gives a more accurate view. Not much sign of a path! There were also no maps. The chief's area you were designated to tour was more a social construct than a defined geographical area, although there might be certain rivers or hills as boundaries. The senior messenger decided the route, and off you went cycling, or in some areas walking from village to village, although here in the Kafue Headwaters there were very few, until you reached the point where the bearers had been sent to make up the next camp. In retrospect it demonstrated our faith in these men.

Another problem on tour was catering, I took my cook with me, but bush catering was a different skill set. For instance, bread was made by digging a hole, filling it with live coals from the fire, then raking them out, inserting dough in a tin with a piece of metal on top covered by more burning embers, sometimes fine but always gritty!

Travelling by road was also not always easy going either, this scene was just prior to the first election arranging for some documents to be delivered to a local chief by his Kapasu, or local police.

After a few months the DC left and I was put in charge. There were regular court sessions which I had to take, mostly minor misdemeanours for which I was authorised to impose a maximum of eighteen months in prison, more usually one or two months. One case did cause me some emotional stress; this was when the European son of a local trader stole a beat up car from a local chief. He appealed my decision and the case was referred to a senior magistrate on where he got off because the victim could not identify the parts stolen. *The bit that catches flies* was not considered a proper legal definition. However the young man had an expensive learning experience, having to pay for a solicitor to avoid conviction, perhaps justice triumphed in spite of the law?

Solwezi had a long tradition of mineral riches. The traditional method of smelting copper was to make little crosses. These were used as currency before the colonial era. Since Independence new mines have been opened in the district.

During my stay in Solwezi the Congo/Katanga was fairly quiet; the border was a line on the map but not clearly marked on the ground. There were markers by the gravel road but nothing else. One track we used on tour weaved across the border as the ground conditions demanded. My messengers regularly patrolled the area, one report read sadly, 'I saw some human bones eaten by animals, a refugee who did not arrive'. We did have one visit from Paramount Chief Mwatiamva form the Congo, which caused some nervousness, would he import the anarchy over the border. In the event all went well, he arrived with some ceremony, presented me with a gift of a vicious panga in a leather scabbard, met the local chiefs and departed. Whatever their allegiance in the past common-sense reigned.

The UN peacekeepers changed on a routine, at New Year it was the Irish with the Rhodesian Army on our side, I did not go to visit but was given to understand that in order to observe the no-fraternising rule, a tent was pitched on the border with a rope down the middle, for New Year celebrations! The next nationality to take over were the Ethiopians, the story was that they were 'disciplined to ferocity'. I never went to meet them.

Later that year the regimental band came to beat the retreat on our football ground, they were in full dress uniform and the ceremony was much enjoyed by a large crowd. In the evening their dance band played for us, the ladies prepared a fine meal, and we took over the DC's spacious house for the event. Very enjoyable until the end when the army driver tried to collect the band in a three ton truck; two problems, he was drunk and the road to the house too narrow, never mind they left in the morning.

One of the delights of Solwezi was the Club. It had various sports facilities, but its main function was the bar; well patronised by the residents. These included a Jesuit mission, the bishop's secretary was a young Irishman, we spent one evening together, a hazy memory probably best forgotten.

At this time we had the first election on a very limited suffrage. I was in charge of a polling station in the south of the district, at a rest camp used for touring. There were only twenty or thirty voters, who all turned up early in the morning, so that bit was easy, the law was for the poll to be open until five, so with the river less than 100 yards down the hill I could spend the rest of the day fishing.

The first moves towards independence were beginning and one project, encouraged by the new PC John Davies, was to try and persuade the local chiefs to think about some

form of local council. Several days of convoluted
discussions followed. They did not want to lose their
authority, UNIP, The United Independence Party were
becoming quite active in the district and were seen as a
threat to traditional values. It was hard to try and sell a
democratic line a very alien concept to traditional rulers.
We did eventually reach some agreement, I was
disappointed but John Davies was complementary, it was
a good first step he said.

By October of 1963 I was beginning to think of plans for
my long leave due in February 1964, sailing home up the
East Coast of Africa, a trip to Israel and maybe time to
learn to ski. Then came a summons to move to Lusaka. My
replacement had arrived but there was no word of what I
was to do next. I duly packed up my kit and drove down to
be told I was to join a team managing the first ever general
election. Quite an exciting project, but I was allocated a
single room in the Government Hostel, a bit of a come
down from my large house in Solwezi, That evening I rang
Richard McVean who I knew had moved from Salisbury to
Lusaka, 'come round for dinner' were his first words. Little
did I know that Pam would be there and my life would
change for ever. Richard had married Frances in Salisbury
and they were living in a pleasant house rented by Anglo
American; he was working as the PA to the Personnel
Director, Pam was the secretary.

Government had fixed at date in February for the election
on universal franchise, it was now October, and we had to
deliver. We were a team of two Richard Marsh in charge
and me, and given office space in a 'tower block', Lusaka's
only one, just four stories tall. There were many
challenges, registration of voters was in train in the

districts, but changes in procedure demanded by politicians caused some headaches. The biggest was the decision to use not just one ballot box per station but one per candidate, so we needed several hundred extra boxes. By good fortune I found a small engineering factory in Lusaka run by an Afrikaner lady who could meet the specification and deliver on schedule. Next the ink used to mark voter's thumbs was not off loaded at Beira, an anxious wait until the arrival of the consignment was confirmed at Dar es Salaam and could be flown down to Lusaka. All was top priority prior to Independence; our office was allowed to use the Government flight to do a circuit of the bush stations to deliver vital documents. Great fun flying in a small plane and seeing the country from above, once I had gained confidence, my assurance was the Australian pilot had a wife and children and intended to get home safely.

Whilst all was happening I could meet Pam most evenings and by Christmas we had become engaged. The official story is that it was on a picnic by the Kafue with the McVeans as he was celebrating the successful launch of a boat he had built. Proposing on the banks of the Kafue makes for a romantic story, but love confuses memory.

The election went well, so my long leave could begin in February. Leaving Pam at work in Lusaka, I flew down to Salisbury to be vetted by Pam's mother – there is evidence she was quite worried! – and her close family friends before catching the train to Beira in Mozambique to join the Europa, an Italian ship bound for Venice. Fortunately I knew nothing of Italian ships, it was just going the right way at the right time; but it was many days before we had a lifeboat drill; the access to the tourist deck was one narrow staircase, and with a large numbers of large Italian mamas dressed all in black, not a happy prospect. It sank a few years later in the Indian Ocean.

With those minor reservations it was an exciting voyage, first port was Dar then Mombasa where HMS Ark Royal was anchored; a platoon of marines had quelled a mutiny in Tanzania a few days earlier, then Aden for some shopping, still a free port. As we went through the Suez Canal I went to Cairo for the museums and the pyramids. Final destination was Venice on a grey cold March morning, then train to Paris and across the Channel home. That year was an early Easter and Pam flew in to join me on the Saturday. A gaggle of relatives came to visit on Easter Monday as we huddled round the fire at Orchards. No sympathy was shown to tropical flowers. Brits are tough, was the message, followed by 'What are you going to do about South Africa'! It was not until the end of that first week of April that the daytime temperature rose above zero. Warm winter coats took priority over buying engagement rings.

English weather, being as ever totally unpredictable, a glorious spring followed; we drove north to see Uncle Dudley and Meg at Southport then down to Devon and Cornwall. My leave was interrupted by a summons to attend the Zambian Independence Conference at Marlborough House; I was put in the Green Park Hotel and given a generous subsistence allowance which paid for Pam's hotel. The duties were not onerous; mainly to ensure the right papers were given to the Zambian delegates to read, Sir Evelyn Hone our Governor and other civil servants collected theirs from the pigeon holes. Every night we went to a show or concert, and Pam had

1. District officer Tony Noel with an assistant and a guard makes election preparations in the Solwezi area

2. Shades of Jack Vettriano ... a couple enjoy a secluded sundowner above the Victoria Falls (Not a posed picture)

3. Lewanika I, the acclaimed and long-serving Litunga of Barotseland

4. Copper smelting in the traditional way. Small copper crosses were currency in pre-colonial times

5.Uniformed messengers take a pride in looking smart

6. The Prophetess Alice Lenshina, who led a rebellion, is received by Tony Noel after her capture

7. Puru, a hand-reared cheetah who acquired a
habit of peering into a bedroom window

8. Water tumbling over the Vic Falls,
with Tony Noel admiring the force

plenty of time to tour Oxford Street for her trousseau. However it did provide an insight into the workings of the British Government; Duncan Sandys presided as Commonwealth Secretary, he was much feared / respected but left to sort out a problem in Aden. The impetus for the talks was when is he due back? The British civil servants clearly had little or no interest in the peoples of Zambia, priorities were 1, how would it be viewed in the UN, 2 in the House, and 3 in Zambia. After all, they were paid by the British taxpayers.

Before we left in May my parents hosted a family party at Orchards, on the lawn under beautiful cherry blossom, Pam was looking her best as we celebrated our engagement with those relatives who would not be able to come to the wedding. Then on the Comet we flew south, celebrations had continued such that somewhere between Rome and Khartoum whilst walking down the aisle to attend a call of nature I slid to the floor. Pam was a trifle suspicious when the air hostess continued to ask after my welfare for the rest of the flight! We landed in Lusaka and Pam was back to the office to tell her boss that it would not be long before she would be leaving.

THIRD TOUR   **Mumbwa -   Broken Hill - UK**

On arrival in Lusaka I was told I was posted to Mumbwa; for us an ideal posting, only two hours' drive from town, so easy to nip in to make arrangements for the wedding, though these mostly fell on Pam's shoulders as she had access to telephones, the line to Mumbwa were erratic at best, although we did have a police radio link to Provincial HQ at Broken Hill.

Mumbwa was an interesting district, then about 40,000 people spread over 8,000 square miles, situated in the Kafue Hook where the river does a huge U bend. To the north it was controlled tsetse country along the river, to the west the Kafue National Park, and to the south the Kafue flats a large area of alluvial flood plain. In the north was a concession originally set aside for potential mining / farming, but never developed. There was one tobacco farmer, Geoff Wedekin, remaining, and also curiously a convent, miles from any villages. The nuns were very hospitable, the Mother superior served tea off Wedgewood china in a Victorian parlour. A few miles north on the river bank was an American Lutheran missionary couple they lived in austere surroundings in isolation from most of the villages.

Mumbwa Boma was on the main road from Lusaka to Mongu, the capital of Barotseland situated on the Zambezi a couple of hundred miles to the west. To the south of the road were three more mission stations, closest was the Methodists, well established with a school and church, very English, make do and mend, no pretensions. A few miles further was another American Lutheran group who lived in rather different style, airstrip and plane and air-conditioned vehicles, no shortage of funds there. Even further down on the Kafue flats another American couple lived in a luxurious bungalow which we visited, Pam long dreamed of having such a superb fitted kitchen. In a relatively small area four versions of Christianity; what did an animist villager make of it all?

The township, several mainly Indian owned shops catering for the locals in the adjacent housing area, was separated from the government offices by a grass airstrip. There was a small hotel run by Jukes Curtis, who also ran a transport business, with his wife Sue, a Kenyan lady who kept a pet cheetah, Puru. They also had a small swimming pool which we used in the hot weather.

Shopping for Pam was not easy 100 miles out in the bush; perishables came weekly in a cool box on the bus. We never had problems, meat was cheap, sometimes we had a whole fillet of beef, it cost a pound! Hard goods we bought on our visits to Lusaka and were kept in a large locked cupboard in the dining room. Inevitably the key was lost one day; not to worry says Kapatula the cook, 'Just shake it and kick it so', it opened. It was only when we returned to UK that we learnt that two people do not drink a pound of tea in a month! How many were we feeding?

The Boma was nearby and the district prison a few hundred yards away. One previous DC had planted a citrus orchard behind the office, which produced a regular supply of grapefruit, there might have been oranges as well but these were all nicked before we could pick them. The DC's house was quite old, relatively small, only two bedrooms but with a guest cottage, all surrounded by mature trees mainly mangoes. The well-established garden included lemons, pawpaw and guava bushes, it faced the airstrip surrounded by frangipani trees, poinsettias and bougainvillea, and a large flame of the forest tree, all in all a very pleasant situation.

When I arrived there was a district officer, John Theakstone, but he was transferred elsewhere quite soon. I do remember one evening we both went out to view an elephant that had been shot near the Boma by a Game Warden. Probably it had been devastating the villagers' fields. It was a sad sight; the locals were beginning to butcher the carcass, but the scale of the body was most repellent. More intimate wild life around the house was the bush babies that lived in the mango trees. They had a noisy social life, courtship necessitated much screaming as they bounced across our corrugated iron roof; then a few weeks later it was time for the kids to leave home, again a very noisy process.

The villagers in the district belonged in the main to the Kaonda tribe, to the north population densities were low, the soil was poor, tsetse flies inhibited the keeping of cattle, but to the south soils were richer, where many Mashona people from Southern Rhodesia had settled. As is frequently the norm, immigrant communities tend to show more initiative than the locals, many had tractors and made a good living from farming. Not surprisingly these tractors and trailers used to transport produce into market in Lusaka broke down frequently, and were then abandoned, making driving at night rather hazardous. As I have mentioned earlier one of the strengths of our district administration throughout NR was the District Messenger team who proudly show off their long service badges as they parade here outside the offices.

One of the delights of Mumbwa was that I did not have to have to take regular court sessions; a resident magistrate came out form Lusaka when necessary to hear any cases. We were now only a few months before Independence so it was a sensitive time, but poaching was on the increase and my messengers were kept busy. One evening they caught the American consul with a warthog in his car. He was highly embarrassed, I took no action beyond confiscating the carcass, but he was worried! I kept a leg which tasted delicious, the chaps enjoyed the rest. To illustrate the scale of the illegal trade, after a few weeks we ended up with seven three-ton trucks full of bush meat, so the prisoners lived well for a while on the fruits of their crimes.

Then in June Pam contracted mumps; very dangerous for young men who had not had the disease in childhood. I stayed well clear until she was declared free of infection and could come out for convalescence. I was banished to the spare room, all doors securely closed and our next wildlife episode began. The mouse or mice that used to roam the house each evening were frustrated and started to noisily nibble a path under the obstacles. Now it was mid-winter, the concrete floors icy to my bare feet, but action was demanded. I failed to make a kill, until one night filling a hot water bottle, half a kettle full of hot water in the other hand, the mouse ran under my feet and got away.

The wedding had been set for August 15, all arrangements made; Pam's boss was also a director of the Ridgeway Hotel, their staff were directed to provide the necessary, whilst the reception was to be held at his new house. He was working on a government salary commission at the time so called for my file to ensure his secretary was marrying a man with good prospects!

Whilst our personal plans were coming to fruition, an insurrection had been taking place 500 miles to the north in Northern Province. A self-styled prophetess Alice Lenshina had visions and her Lumpa followers had violent confrontations with the police and army causing considerable loss of life. Finally she had been captured

with her husband, and on Tuesday, August 14, I was
informed my prison would be her place of detention. All
the prisoners and the confiscated lorries were taken away,
and on Thursday Alice arrived in a plane marked Zambian
Air Force, two months prior to Independence!

Together with my Messengers I was on the airstrip to
welcome her; there was quite a crowd of onlookers; top
brass from Lusaka including unbeknown to me the press.
This resulted in me being headlined on the front page of
the Northern News next morning, Friday, August 14,
causing great consternation to Pam, her mother and my
parents gathering for our wedding the following day! The
headline was HER WORRIES ARE OVER. Pam was not
quite so sure, not having heard from me for several days.

Having settled Alice, her husband and two small children
into the prison, I spoke with the Provincial Commissioner,
who told me to go off for my wedding, his next words were
'Where is the key for the boat?' a twelve foot metal dingy
with outboard which we kept on the Kafue. I then drove
into Lusaka, initially to the VW garage where I exchanged
my green model for a new blue one, and then to meet Pam,
who was much relieved to see me.
That evening we had a family dinner arranged by Pam's
mother for all involved in the wedding celebrations; my
parents and cousin Janet, family and friends from
Salisbury, including Elspeth Lawrence and her parents,
and several others, a splendid affair. That night I was to
stay in the Lusaka Hotel on Cairo Road until the ceremony
on the Saturday afternoon. The morning passed in a whirl
but eventually I was delivered to the Church on time by
Mark Sheldrake, who I had met in Katete where he was
doing VSO, as the best man, he had travelled from

Shesheke in Barotseland by boat and train to be there. The wedding was conducted by Rev J Fields at the Methodist Church on the Ridgeway just below the Cathedral, the service began with the Hymn, Praise my Soul, now sung at all our family events; whilst we signed the register Elspeth who had been at school with Pam sang, How Blessed are the Feet, from Handel's Messiah.

We were about forty guests in all, who then drove the short distance to Dennis Etheridge's house for the reception in his garden, fortunately it was a pleasant warm evening, Dudley Lawrence spoke, he had known Pam since childhood and I mumbled a few words of thanks to all. We were spending our first night together at the Ridgeway Hotel, but were so tired that we did not go into dinner. In retrospect it might be that the four dozen bottles of South African 'champagne' for forty guests could have been a factor.

The next morning we drove to Livingstone to spend our honeymoon at the Victoria Falls Hotel. As we drove out of the car park we noticed a green VW identical to my old car daubed with streamers and so forth, there was no other wedding in town that day, so someone was mightily embarrassed! At Victoria Falls we spent an idyllic week, one evening meeting Mark and Jan in the middle of the bridge as we took an after dinner stroll.
Then all too soon we had to drive back to Mumbwa to entertain my parents who had been spending time touring in in the mountains of Southern Rhodesia. They had yet to experience real Africa. Now our generator had been moved to the prison, we had only Tilley lamps and candles; the woodstove which went out after dinner was cooked, a bit tricky when late evening cups of tea were requested. We

picked them up in Lusaka and drove 100 miles home, about two hours, but their first experience of gravel roads. Next morning mother woke up with a headache, 'I need to see a doctor'. Fine we will drive back to Lusaka and arrange it, 'Not along that awful road', she got better quickly, but so it went on for a difficult fortnight. One day we drove them up to the National Park to look at game another day was spent on the Kafue in our little boat. Mother was in a constant state of terror but Father got confident and wanted close ups of hippos; he could not comprehend how dangerous they could be. I think they enjoyed the experience in retrospect, but they found coping with the dust difficult on the bush roads. They flew home on the 'school flight' surrounded by children returning to boarding school in early September. They took many mixed memories of NR home to Orchards.

Then it was back to the routines, Alice was settled in the prison with her family, and district affairs continued with little change; however we did have a prison officer to manage the place, one less job for my messengers.

I had several chats with Alice, her husband Petros, and her children, seemingly such ordinary villagers; it was hard to imagine the power and authority she had wielded. Yet the fatalities were a reality, over 500. I remain convinced that the situation could have been peacefully managed if the passions of Independence had not intervened.

Geoff Wedekin invited us for a weekend to visit his farm; his wife was away in Kenya, it was corned beef for lunch, dinner, and probably breakfast, washed down with Lanzerac Rose, a rather sweet South African wine we enjoyed at the time. The first problem arose when Pam decided to have a bath, she found the pet otter sleeping in it, it was the size of a large labrador with teeth to match, the staff were summoned, and it was evicted. Then to bedtime, when the houseboy came in with a large macaw on a broom stick, the bird slept in a tea chest mounted above the double bed. This was a traditional homemade bed of local wood with reams, ancient cured leather thongs instead of springs, these had stretched over time. It was kind of Geoff to give up his bed for us!

The next visit to his farm was at Christmas time, his wife was back and we had all the trimmings for dinner, all went well until the macaw and the otter had a fight under Pam's chair! All three took off in different directions, the macaw now reduced to one tail feather! Then, as the mince pies were circulating the pet hartebeest grabbed one off the plate, she slapped his nose and quickly put it back on the plate, strangely no one else wanted one after that.

By October it was very hot, The Prison Officer, a typical tough South African, had a large Boxer dog and a visiting glamorous girlfriend, they were relaxing by the Hotel pool and we were there too. The girl was in the water, dog decided to join her, then Puru the cheetah, came past decided to chase the dog and jumped in too. Macho prison officer jumped to rescue his girl so the pool was getting crowded. We were hysterical with laugher, the girl was first out! It was a few mornings later when Pam opened the curtains to see Puru peering in our bedroom window.

At the end of October it was Independence time; we had been allocated large boxes of fireworks, as many as our budget could stand; there was much excitement that evening, sweet and sour because I knew that my time at Mumbwa was limited. I had made a decision to resign at the end of 1965 to start a new career before reaching thirty, but in the meantime life and work continued as normal.

One evening we were entertaining some visiting local chiefs and dignitaries including a High Court Judge; Pam must have been looking weary so he came up to her and said 'Do you want to get rid of them now, He promptly went the rounds shaking hands and saying 'good night'; within a few minutes they had all gone and we could sit down to dinner. It was a masterly performance.

Before Christmas when Richard, Frances and baby Andrea came to stay, we had managed a couple of weekend trips, firstly to the Kafue National Park as an extension of our brief honeymoon; then later to Salisbury to visit Pam's mother, where l we bought the lovely Joan Evans painting, that hangs in our lounge, it is so evocative of springtime in central Africa, when the leaves come out in beautiful colours in the summer heat, before the rains before the rains begin.

More dramatic perhaps a test of our wedding vows was a police exercise along the Kafue. The police training party had borrowed the boat as they went on a trek, an early essay into Outward Bound training, along the river. I had agreed to go down and bring the boat back, some ten miles or maybe more. We found them easily, a bit scared as lions had been around during the night, I started up the outboard and decided to do a bit of fishing while it was cool. Pam and I caught several bream but then a herd of elephants crossed the river quite close, there were also hippos nearby; it was time to go. By now the engine was less cooperative and would not start. We paddled to the side, still the engine would not start, so I decided to walk and catch up the police party. By now it was hot, we had one messenger with us but the police party had kept hold of the rifle, thinking about the lions. The first few hundred yards were like a muddy farmyard backed dry, except it was elephant feet that made the holes. I think we walked for about an hour before we met the party camping for lunch; this was definitely Pam's first experience of drinking tea from a billycan, and in the circumstances very enjoyable! The marriage survived.

The New Year began with the news of Churchill's death. To me this symbolised the end of an era. Many of the messengers had war service and could understand my feelings. Routines in the district had changed little after Independence, various senior politicians came to visit and be entertained, but life went on much as normal.Then in April my replacement arrived, he spoke little English and showed no interest as I tried to explain the workings of the district, obviously a party hack drawing his reward. I just felt so sorry for the staff I had to leave behind and who had worked so loyally for many years. I was transferred to a non-job in Broken Hill, where we stayed until my resignation became effective in October, a very boring and depressing time. There was much that could have been done, but the new Zambian PC seemed not to trust the competence of the remaining district officers and was just waiting for us to go.

Finally all the boxes were packed and put on the train for Cape Town Docks; with one exception, foolishly most of the wedding presents and table linen, some belonging to

Pam's grandmother, were all in one crate, this was almost certainly stolen at Broken Hill on 'insider information'. We went from twenty something sets of table napkins to none!

It was late in October that we flew down to Salisbury to stay with Pam's mother for a few days. Whilst there I went to the Native Affairs Department to find out if there were any job prospects in Southern Rhodesia. The chap I met made it crystal clear they were not interested, and their philosophy was control not development. A day or two later whilst we were in a coffee shop in central Salisbury Ian Smith came on the radio to make his Unilateral Declaration of Independence speech. Everyone in the shop listened attentively then burst out cheering at the end. For Pam and me it was a very sad moment, but we dared not show our feelings of anxiety for the future amidst such euphoria. It was fifty years later before I again had the same feeling of apprehension; the morning after the Brexit vote was declared. At a more simplistic personal level I was waiting on a sale price for the car I had left in Zambia and worried about a slump in second-hand car prices.

After a few more days we said our farewells went, to the railway station and boarded the train for Cape Town, a three day journey south. We stayed in Cape Town for about a week, travelled around the Cape visiting beaches, Table Mountain and Kirstenbosch Gardens before boarding the SS Vaal for the voyage home.

We were allocated a superb cabin on the boat deck of this one class ship, because we were out of season, heading into the winter in UK. Pam had altered her wedding dress into this magnificent outfit for the Captain's cocktail party and I had bought a dinner jacket for the voyage. It mouldered in a cupboard when we got back to normal life, but we made the most of the voyage.

It was a cold December morning when we docked in Southampton; my parents met us at the quayside and we drove to Orchards just in time for Christmas. Pam was three months pregnant with Christopher, I had no job, not the easiest of times.

New Year 1965 presented a few challenges, no job, no home and pregnant wife. First stop was the resettlement bureau, who suggested a business studies course in the City, then job hunting, all the advice pointed to a role in personnel, manpower resources in today's language. I thought I needed to learn a bit about business first so opted for Organisation and Methods focusing on office functions as a start point. Sainsbury made an offer contingent on attending a course run by ICI in May, so I chose them and started in April.

Meantime we had taken a short term let on a flat in Henley; we had bought a Mini Minor so Pam was mobile, although she had to take another driving test. It was no surprise when they drove past the maternity hospital that the examiner called for the emergency stop! He needed reassurance. House hunting could begin now I had a place of work established, Walton was the first place on the line into Waterloo, too expensive for our budget, then Woking, where we found a new house almost finished and made an offer. I had a resettlement grant from the government and my father generously topped this up. We, or rather I, moved in on a Saturday in June, Christopher had arrived during the night, so after staying with Pam for the birth I

met a removal van at Orchards and moved into Triggs
Close that day.

Pam stayed in hospital for a week, and it was the following
weekend when the family could move in. So a new phase of
our family life began that weekend of June 11-12, 1964.
Less adventurous maybe, but full of demands and rewards
for us both as new parents, starting a new job in UK on
less than half the pay I had earned as a DC with a season
ticket to buy and income tax to pay.

NEWS MEDIA IN KAUNDA'S ZAMBIA AND AFTER: 1973 - 1995

(Extracted from *Journalism My Way*, by Cedric Pulford (Ituri, 2013)

I didn't know it at the time, but Lagos in 1972 was famous as one of the most difficult cities in Africa: perpetual traffic jams, water, electricity and telephones forever failing – and all topped off by a flood of refugees from the recently concluded Biafran War and the punishing humidity of the West Coast.

Seven months later, in Zambia, I could hardly believe how different it was. The jacaranda trees were in full bloom when I arrived in Lusaka, the capital, to run a month-long course in journalism – street upon street of glorious purple blossoms. The streets themselves were wide and, away from the Cairo Road shopping district, almost empty. The place seemed to operate in an ordered way.

Lusaka has one of the world's most pleasant climates. At more than three-quarters of a mile above sea level (4,265ft or 1,300m), it is hot but without the enervating humidity of the coastal areas. The seasons are varied enough to keep things interesting.

The tutor team for the course was my fellow Thomson Foundation staffer, Norman Cattanach, and myself. Norman, who had been chief sub-editor of the South Wales Echo, went on to a distinguished career in training. He ran the in-house journalism scheme for the Straits Times in Singapore, where he recanted his previous life running short courses of the type we were engaged in. He described them dismissively as 'flying workshops'. In due time, he found himself the director of the foundation – when presumably he recanted his recantation.

We stayed at the Ridgeway Hotel, where the terrace was built around a pond. I was enchanted by the weaver birds busy with their nest building. The Ridgeway was owned by Anglo-American, the dominant force in the copper mining that made Zambia wealthy. The editors' committee organising the course gave us a car for our exclusive use for the month. This was unthinkable on my many later visits to the country, as the economy deteriorated.

Zambia was on the way to becoming a one-party state under Kenneth Kaunda's United National Independence Party. Of the two daily newspapers, the Zambia Daily Mail was owned by the government. The other, older newspaper was the Times of Zambia. It had a bigger circulation and was owned by Lonrho, a conglomerate with businesses throughout Africa. It too had links with government: the editor was Vernon Mwanga, a former minister. When Kaunda instituted the one-party state, the Times was nationalised.

Radio and television were also state-owned. There was no satellite TV in those days and short-wave radio could be erratic. The internet was more than two decades in the future. Thus the Zambian public had few opportunities to hear other views than the government's. The newspapers were freer than the broadcast media. They did an adequate job in providing 'bread and butter' domestic news, and were quite adept in presenting foreign news from the agencies. They were weakest with the dug out material that is to be found 'off diary' – stories that don't come from press releases, press conferences or official announcements. The importance of active news in this sense was one of the issues we took up on the course. This was a seminar-workshop held in ideal circumstances. Around a dozen journalists took part from all parts of the media. It was held in stylish Mulungushi Hall, which had been recently built for an international meeting of African officials.

Despite Norman's later doubts about 'flying workshops', I felt confident that some of the course insights would prove lasting. The poet Edmund Blunden said that one poem could justify a lifetime. The same can be said of a month-long training course if participants come away with a single, game-changing insight.

Some of the 1973 course participants were at the top of Zambian media when I worked in the country twenty years later. Sadly, one of the brightest, Emmanuel Chayi, died after he had become the director-general of Zambia Broadcasting Corporation, a casualty of the Aids epidemic.

Nineteen seventy-five found me back in Zambia, this time in the idyllic setting of the Mindolo Ecumenical Centre at Kitwe on the Copperbelt. Tropical flowers blazed forth their colours in winter temperatures of around 30C. Tea was taken on the lawn, mornings and afternoons. I was allocated a bungalow and a vehicle for my month-long stay as a guest lecturer and consultant with the centre's offshoot, the Africa Literature Centre (ALC).

All was not as comfortable as it seemed, however. This was a time of severe food shortages in Zambia. As part of the boycott of apartheid South Africa, President Kaunda had closed the Zimbabwe (then Rhodesia) border through which most imports had arrived. Much of the day was taken up with looking for food staples. A message would arrive on the bush telegraph, 'There's bread at ...' or ' ... has sugar' and off we'd go. I suppose Mindolo engaged in collective buying because students didn't go short of food, but other campus residents like me fended for ourselves. Mindolo was where I encountered sliced avocado being ladled from a large bowl in the canteen, in the manner of cabbage at my English school. Truly, other places, other customs (and other costs)!

The ALC director was E.C. (Zeke) Makunike, a Zimbabwean and former magazine editor and director of Methodist Publications in Rhodesia. The head of journalism was Michael Traber, a Swiss Roman Catholic priest, also a former magazine editor and director of Mambo Press, Rhodesia. Although the centre had a chronic lack of lecturers, the agreeable Zeke didn't do any teaching. One of my main recommendations in due course was that he should put aside any considerations of status, and pitch in. Unfortunately, this sense of hierarchy was too common in Africa.

Mike Traber had the best command of English I've ever met in a non-native speaker. His vocabulary and grasp of idioms were astonishing. He wore his clericalism lightly, and his priestly dress not at all. Only once did his Catholicism burst out. I'd made some remark about Anglicans, and he spat: 'That heretic church!'

The Africa Literature Centre's programmes had been strongly criticised the year before (1974) separately by three visiting consultants: my Thomson Foundation colleague, John Cardownie; a training warhorse and International Press Institute stalwart, Frank Barton; and John Musukuma, the ablest Zambian journalist of his generation.

Part of the issue was that Zeke and Mike's backgrounds weren't sufficiently hard-edged for newspapers and broadcasting as well as magazines; secular media as well as religious media. In consequence, the courses weren't rigorous enough. A comment from one of the visiting examiners sums it up: 'Less than five students [out of 19] showed evidence in their examination papers that they had learnt anything from the course - if there was anything to learn from it.'

Zeke and Mike to their credit wished to raise standards. Mike had visited the Thomson Foundation centre in Cardiff to observe the training techniques in use there; now I was assigned to the ALC for a month to inject 'the Thomson touch'.

As always, I stressed the need for practicality: mass communication theory to be retained but given in the latter part of the course; African ideologies to be spread throughout the course rather than delivered in indigestible lumps. The course timetable was to be based on the talk-do-discuss sequence. The general standard of English on the present course was poor. I urged compulsory English lessons for two hours a day at first, phasing out over the six-month programme. A student from Portuguese West Africa (Angola) had practically no English. It was impossible to help him, but the others were from Anglophone countries – Uganda, Tanzania, Malawi, South

Africa and Zambia itself – and would benefit from the forcing-house approach.

Zeke Makunike and Mike Traber in a letter of appreciation were kind enough to describe my ideas as 'most valuable innovations', citing the areas of course programming, lecture preparation and presentation, content of exercises and tutorial administration. The Africa Literature Centre month had been a learning experience for me, too, in my dual role of guest lecturer and consultant adviser. In Nigeria, I had been a guest lecturer but made little impact as an adviser. Now, with three years' experience and a hard journalism background I had the confidence to bring about improvements.

I had got to know Colonel Terence Pierce-Goulding, the secretary (later styled director) of the Commonwealth Press Union, when I was at the Thomson Foundation. The CPU was an association of newspaper proprietors from around the Commonwealth, run from a tiny office under the eaves of a Dickensian building in Fleet Street. In summer this was known as the 'CPU sauna'.

When in 1979 Terry sent me on my first assignment as a CPU consultant, it was back to Zambia. I felt at home on this my third visit. Again, I marvelled at the spaciousness of the capital, Lusaka. It was no wonder that it had room to spread: the city was established on the open savannah because it was the midway point on the railway between the Victoria Falls and the Copperbelt. It took its name from the nearby kraal of a local chief.

The Ridgeway Hotel was in the 'government area', about a mile from the business district of Cairo Road. This reflected the social divide in colonial times between the officials and the traders. Beyond Cairo Road was the third element in the demographic makeup, a shantytown for the urban poor. It wasn't extensive in those days, but I was to see it grow hugely over the years. These shantytowns are often forgotten when we speak of life in Africa and the Majority World generally. They are neither urban nor rural: they are in the city but not fully of it.

If my work for the next six weeks was familiar, there was a new element to this training workshop. I was alone. It was hard work with no-one to share the teaching or the course organisation. It gave added piquancy to the sundowner, the welcome first drink at the end of the day in that brief, magical time before the African sun disappeared.

I remember especially the magical evening when on a visit to the Victoria Falls I had the falls to myself. It was sundown and no one was about in the garden of the tourist lodge. It was a few hundred yards above the falls. I took a table at the edge of the Zambezi, lingered over a beer and marvelled at the spray rising above the lip of the cataract after dashing on the rocks 355ft (100m) below. In fact, the wall of spray can reach 1,000ft (300m).

The falls are twice as deep as Niagara, and at 5,500ft (1,675m) far wider. They are known to the local Lozi tribe as Mosi-oa-Tunya ('The Smoke That Thunders'), a name sensibly adopted for the nearby hotel on the Zambian side. Visitors to Vic Falls stand at the edge and look down at the rainbow. Nor is it a fugitive band of dissipated light. It is substantial enough to snap and show the people back home.

I've been fortunate to visit the Victoria Falls several times. I found the undeveloped Zambian side peaceful and relaxing. It was so unlike the crowds and the hustling on the Zimbabwe side (where I saw a package tourist with his feet on the table in the formerly select Victoria Falls Hotel).

My overseas work mainly lay in capital cities, but wherever possible I got out to see something of the country. Often I extended my stay privately. I never understood many of my colleagues, who, finding themselves at no expense to themselves in some of the world's most interesting places, could think only of getting home again. Sometimes I had to discourage colleagues from leaving on the same evening that the course ended, which was a discourtesy to our hosts.

Taking photographs in public places was risky in Zambia at that time. The authorities were edgy about security because of Kaunda's confrontation with South Africa and Rhodesia. They feared that spies were everywhere. Not only was the border sealed for South African goods but also Zambia hosted the guerrilla training camps of Joshua Nkomo's ZAPU. (Robert Mugabe's ZANU was based in Mozambique.) Not being a war correspondent, I've heard shots fired in anger only once. This was when aircraft of the Rhodesian air force shot up the camps near Lusaka.

I hated to be thwarted of what I foolishly saw as my divine right to take pictures where I pleased. I was snapping away in the street in Kitwe on the Copperbelt when an expatriate pulled his car over and gave me a friendly warning. Didn't I know that people were arrested for doing that? Stupidly, I gave him a graceless reply and carried on. On that occasion nothing happened.

I was taking a photograph of Lusaka's new Pamodzi Hotel when I was stopped by a man who said he was a plain-clothes policeman. His manner suggested that it wasn't a good idea to argue, or even to demand his ID. He was all too believable. He demanded my camera, ripped out the entire roll of film thus destroying the images, handed the camera back and walked on. In the circumstances I got off lightly.

The government launched newspapers in four or five vernacular languages to expand literacy in the rural areas. This worthy objective ran into the central difficulty of a lack of books and other reading matter in the indigenous languages. An adviser told me that without fresh material to tackle, reading skills erode. I learnt that reading isn't like riding a bicycle: once you can do it, you can do it forever. If you don't keep reading, you will eventually forget how.

By 1986 I was on my sixth assignment in Zambia, most of them training workshops for all sections of the news media. I was well aware of the strengths and weaknesses. The media were relatively sophisticated, which I liked to think was something to do with the huge training effort poured into the country. At the same time, it was on a tight leash with all principal outlets controlled by the ruling party, President Kenneth Kaunda's UNIP, or the government (effectively the same thing in a one-party state). This situation had got worse when the Times of Zambia, previously owned by Lonrho, had been taken over by the state. The system wasn't overtly oppressive, but freedom of speech was limited by self-censorship – arguably the severest censorship of all. It would have been impossible, for example, to challenge the idea of the one-party state or to dispute Kaunda's policy of boycotting South Africa.

Shoots of spring were to be seen, however. The private and irreverent Weekly Post appeared. Aware that journalists wished to turn the political climate to advantage, I decided to speak out in an article in the Times of Zambia (SEE ANNEXE TO THIS ARTICLE)..

Zambia had made a good start, I argued, but liberalisation needed to be speeded up if its news media were to take their rightful place at the centre of a free society. The government owned both national dailies. I saw no reason why the government shouldn't own a daily paper, but to own both was one too many. The papers should be privatised, and a press council set up to guarantee standards.

The national news agency could be handed over to the Zambian media. The system by which new publications had to be registered should be scrapped, with a press council set up to safeguard standards. The state still had to get its message across. Zambia Information Services (ZIS) should stay in government hands.
 An unmuzzled media would be a step forward in Zambia's development, enabling members of the modern elite – civil servants, business people, white-collar workers – to communicate with each other and, equally importantly, with the government.

I was keen to acknowledge that the requirements of the media were different in advanced and emerging countries, and that there were reasons why well intentioned governments used the state control model, however deficient it proved to be in practice. I was equally keen to stress that the model should no longer be used to deny educated urban dwellers in a place like Zambia what they desired as strongly as their Western counterparts: a free press.

That article was a courageous piece to run. But the courage was not mine – as an expatriate consultant the worst likely penalty would be to be on the next plane out – but that of the editors of the Times of Zambia. It was an encouraging sign of Zambia's progress to press freedom that they felt able to do so after the long years of self-censorship.

In Zambia and over much of the Majority World, the dominance of the Big Four news agencies meant that international news was presented through Western eyes. Jeremy Tunstall, a British media sociologist, wrote an influential book titled *The Media Are American*. Two of the agencies, Associated Press and United Press International, were American; the two others, Reuters and Agence France-Presse were heavily influenced by America.

This led to the phenomenon of agenda setting, in which newspapers and broadcasters around the world absorb and reflect the news values of the agencies without adaptation to their own customers. The agencies didn't set out to project a jingoistic Western or specifically American news agenda, but they were naturally focused on their primary markets.
Particularly in Africa, supplementary sources of international news were hard to find. The main issue, however, was the mindset of journalists in the Majority

World. In country after country in Africa, Asia and the Caribbean, I urged editors to make their own judgements in terms of their readers, not blindly follow the priorities of the agency.

For instance, a coup in South America meant less in Asia than it did in adjacent Hispanic countries, so why run many paragraphs on a story whose local news value was three or four paragraphs? My special bugbear was saturation coverage of US domestic politics, which tended to be printed at a length that few readers wanted, just because an agency sent it that way. Sadly, most journalists lacked the confidence to decide for themselves. If AP puts a certain weight on a story, it must be so ...

In 1991 the mood in Zambia was that President Kaunda's government – in power since independence almost three decades before – had overstayed its time. With the economy on the floor and with the suffering that brought, the people demanded change. I returned to the country that year. The coming change was palpable. The flags of Frederick Chiluba's Movement for Multiparty Democracy were everywhere. Children flashed the MMD hand sign to cars as they passed by.

The MMD was swept to power in the election and Kaunda, to his credit, stood down graciously. I too was caught up in the mood for change. Of course, with hindsight it was naive to expect a new heaven and a new earth. The new government was a shaky coalition of business and labour interests. The new president – a tiny man in contrast to Kaunda, who was above average height – was the former trade union chief. The independent Weekly Post was later to describe Chiluba as 'a product of Kaunda's repression', a man whose 'credibility begins and ends with Kaunda'.

It was, however, significant that the new climate of free speech allowed the Post to make such a comment with impunity. For all that, the MMD was soon mired in difficulties – some produced by carrying out Western-induced structural adjustment programmes and others, like drug trafficking in the top reaches of government, defections and corruption, home-made. Crime soared as salaries failed to cover bare necessities and there was hunger in parts of the countryside. The average clerk earned the equivalent of only US$45 a month. But the government brought once-runaway inflation under control. Goods were in the shops for those who could afford them.

I was in Zambia for the Friedrich Naumann Stiftung (Foundation), having been recruited to run a one-month training workshop by the station chief, Hartmut Giering. FNF was the development agency of Germany's Free Democratic Party. This was the start of an agreeable five-year association that ended when Hartmut resigned and went to Zimbabwe to run a tourist lodge. He and I remained good friends afterwards.

By now I had trained a substantial chunk of Zambia's press corps. Some had risen to high positions, including Cyrus Sikazwe, editor in chief of the Times of Zambia, Josephine Mapoma, permanent secretary at the Ministry of Information and Broadcasting, and Patrick Nkama, an editorial executive at the Zambia Daily Mail. Others had left the profession, persuaded by the better money to be had in public relations or private business.

Returning to Zambia annually for five years in the Nineties, I found a very different country from the one I had known. Yet in 1993, two years after the MMD came to power, the country's state-controlled news media were still struggling to find a new role.

Expression was far freer than under Kaunda. Newspapers and television covered all political parties, and vigorous views not always to the government's liking were found in articles and readers' letters. But ministerial rhetoric and non-story ceremonies remained strongly in evidence on news pages and even more on TV and radio – the familiar recipe from one-party state days.

Discouragingly for supporters of independent media, President Chiluba's government seemed to be in no hurry to give up any of its media, which included the country's two daily newspapers. Nor did it show signs of ending practices like the registration of publications or filtering the output of foreign news agencies like Reuters and Agence France-Presse through the state-owned Zambia News Agency (ZANA).

The government's stance appeared to be that so long as anyone else could start a newspaper there was no reason why it should not keep the two it owned. And if the Times of Zambia and the Zambia Daily Mail were put up for sale it was not clear whether anyone would want to buy them. They had large staffs and obsolete equipment and a combined daily sale in a nation of 8½ million of under 50,000 copies.
Meanwhile, the independent Weekly Post, which started in the late Kaunda days, was believed to have overtaken the Times as the nation's biggest-selling newspaper. The Post

was vigorous, annoying and stimulating. It linked Princess Nakatindi Wina, a government minister, with allegations of drug smuggling and financial corruption – the type of story that would have been impossible over much of the Majority World.

Managing director Fred M'membe received the attentions of the police over a leaked cabinet document. It was one of several such encounters, but the paper continued to appear freely on the streets.

Low newspaper sales reflected the fact that for many Zambians – beset at that time by soaring inflation and the austerities of structural adjustment imposed by the World Bank and the International Monetary Fund – a newspaper had become a luxury. It wasn't always so. A striking feature of Zambia in the Seventies was vendors doing bumper sales in the streets. Yet for the would-be press baron underlying factors remained good: national adult literacy at 73 per cent and urbanisation at 56 per cent – both high for Africa.

Ex-President Kaunda was having difficulty in coming to terms with his loss of power after twenty-seven years. He told a rally in his stronghold Eastern Province that he was giving the nation two months to decide if it wanted him back, and that Zambians did not 'have to wait until 1996' (the next elections) to change the government. This was read as an invitation to unconstitutional action, but the MMD government, probably not wanting to make a martyr of Kaunda, responded only with words. And it soon became clear that voters did not need two months to consider Kaunda's offer. Public reaction was generally hostile.

A few days later Kaunda appeared to retract. He said he had been misquoted at the rally, and an accurate statement had been blocked. Then he repositioned himself by telling businessmen that centralist economic planning had outlived its usefulness. Africa should embrace free market economics. Bar-room pundits joked that Kaunda could come back under the government banner.

I turned road-going reporter to follow up the story for the Observer News Service, helped by the fact that everyone spoke English. On the streets of Lusaka it was hard to find anyone who supported a comeback by Kaunda. Grace Phiri, a pavement vendor, said: 'He was a good president. He felt for the people. But his time has gone. Let him rest.' Student Bridget Phiri dismissed him with a sarcastic reference to his advancing years: 'He is my grandfather. If Chiluba has failed, there are others.'

Many Zambians blamed Kaunda for the ramshackle economy. The feeling that he had no right to question the activities of the present government underpinned many of the criticisms. Electrician Jovito Jere said Kaunda failed to make things work in twenty-seven years, and asked, 'What has changed?' Samson Chama, an airline worker, was more impassioned: 'He left a legacy of utter destruction. Now he wants to return, claim credit for it, and then destroy again what someone else has tried to rebuild.'

Zambians were puzzled about why Kaunda should want to come back at all, with his valuable retirement package – a pension, a new home in a location of his choice, transport, office staff and security – and continued international prominence. The impoverished nation was a small bottle of Mosi (the local beer) compared with the global stage, where

Kaunda enjoyed the friendship of South African president Nelson Mandela. Yet few politicians like to contemplate a career ending in failure, particularly those with the brio to say, as Kaunda did, 'I built this country and I can't destroy it'.

The long Kaunda administration was once widely popular for its progressive policies and commitment to welfare. But with a leader who was often preoccupied with African liberation abroad, it ended with food shortages, soaring prices, padded public payrolls, a disintegrating economy and a pre-revolutionary mood in the country.

Under the one-party state, restrictions on the news media were never total and bar talk flowed; yet the regime practised political repression and even torture – a point that President Chiluba was quick to pick up on. The tragedy of Kaunda is that he came to preside over a regime with a mixed record on human rights – the very issue that won him his international reputation.

Zambia's economic austerity programme spawned a growing army of street children. I interviewed a number of them. Agnes, aged seven, sold unappetising wares from a makeshift stand. The fruits, fried groundnuts and roast meats were covered in dust, with flies alighting here and there. She had no knowledge of food hygiene, but nor did her only customers – other street kids – so perhaps it didn't matter too much.

At ten, Katandula was already sexually experienced. Her customers were older street kids who had graduated to the status of 'mishanga' boys, the dubious characters whose activities ranged from hawking cigarettes to stealing them and anything else. If Katandula was typical, by the age of fourteen she would have borne an unwanted child; at twenty she would be dead from Aids in a country where HIV infected at least a quarter of the urban population.

At least adult Zambians knew they were suffering the pain of structural adjustment in the hope of eventual gain. Street kids knew only that they suffered.

Boys as young as six were to be seen on the streets. Some just wandered around near restaurants in the hope of leftovers. Outside an eating place in Kamwala township a pack of boys squatted. Whenever a customer threw some food, it was snatched up by the eldest boy and the rest got none. Eventually all drifted away except the youngest, aged around seven. Calling himself Jimmy, the boy told his tale. He said he had never seen his father, and his mother was out with men during the day and only returned at night. 'I usually pick my food on the streets,' Jimmy started to explain, 'because there is nothing to eat at home and my mother beats me when ...' Before he could finish, an Asian appeared from the restaurant and threw an eggroll at the boy. Jimmy snatched the food and retreated to the nearest gutter. He appeared again after a minute or so licking his lips and ran for home.

Unlike Jimmy, many boys and girls had no home except the streets. If there could be degrees of sadness in such a situation perhaps the saddest were those like Jimmy, who had a home of sorts, but who had to roam the streets to find the basics the home did not supply.

Of course, there were charitable organisations trying to help. But, lacking funds, they were like an army of determined soldiers without guns.

The Family Health Trust focused on orphans, whose parents in most cases had died from Aids. John Munsanjc, manager of the trust's Children in Distress department, reported surprisingly: 'Children, especially orphans, go to the streets because that is where they seem to get love and solace.' He and his colleagues tried to give that support in more benign ways, feeding the children and sending them to school until they had a chance to fend for themselves.

At the Zambia Red Cross Society's day centre in Lusaka's Garden Compound, children aged between five and eighteen were taught carpentry, brick-making, tailoring and homecraft as well as school subjects. A spokeswoman regretted that a 'get rich quick' attitude among many Zambians was threatening the charitable support on which the centre depended. She said: 'No one is ready to share what he has with a neighbour. One would rather see his friend die than give a helping hand.'

The Human Rights Association of Zambia formed a club to teach street kids practical skills. Trustee Mrs Maureen Mainbwe said: 'It is painful to see innocent young children roaming the street with nothing to do when they should be in school. However, parents cannot afford the fees.' Concerned adults wished more companies would follow the example of Armcor Security, which recruited more than twenty ex-street kids who had been rehabilitated at the Red Cross centre.

The government, meanwhile, was lacking in serious action. With growing unemployment, continuing though slowing inflation, a crumbling manufacturing sector and all-but-invisible tourism, it seemed to have no energy left for the street kids.

ANNEXE: PRESS FREEDOM IN THE MAJORITY WORLD
Article by Cedric Pulford in the Times of Zambia, 1993

The liberalisation of the news media in Zambia is part of a global process that is sweeping vast areas including Africa, Eastern Europe and South America into democracy. Even before this rush of political pluralism, the idea of State control of the media was losing its grip in Zambia and other countries because of its deficiencies in practice.

Whatever the myth of everyone pulling together for the Great Upward Heave, people in the modern sector of Third World countries have always been just as keen on an independent press as their counterparts in the advanced countries. Want it and need it, for muzzled media do not allow the elites – the entrepreneurs, professionals, academics, civil servants, managers and teachers – to communicate properly, and nor do governments get vital feedback.

The state control model of the press devised by developmental theorists in the Fifties and Sixties had a respectable pedigree, but it never delivered. As countries like Kenya, Singapore and South Korea have shown over the years, increasing economic development does not necessarily produce the predicted easing of shackles on the press.

So by now a free press is the only credible model in the market place. What does it say, and what might it mean for Zambia?

In a pluralistic democracy the news media and the government are seen as separate pillars of the free society. The whole edifice is weakened if the pillars are joined together. This means there can be no proper place for the registration or licensing of publications, or for a state-controlled news agency monopolising incoming wire services and redistributing a selected file to the media organisations.

New publications still have to be registered in Zambia and ZANA [Zambia News Agency] continues to redistribute Reuters, Agence-France Presse and the other external agencies. Because media and government are separate pillars of democracy there is a presupposition against the state controlling newspapers (I will come to broadcasting in a moment). This does not mean that the government cannot own a paper, but in the Zambian situation the government would surely lose credibility with international donors and investors if it continues to own both daily newspapers.

People buy newspapers for three main reasons: To make money, for social prestige (you are seen as a more interesting person if you own a newspaper than a textile mill) and to make propaganda. The last point can clearly be a problem: If government is not to regulate the content of news media, that does not mean no-one else should. A press council operating a code of conduct is the best way to maintain acceptable standards of independent media. A fundamental issue is whether such an ethical body is to be government-created with statutory powers, or operated by the media industry and journalistic profession based on voluntary compliance. The former is more potent but risks state control by the back-door. If Zambia introduces a code of conduct for news media, I hope the voluntary route will he tried first.

Ethical codes are not solely about control, however. They also permit journalists to do things. For instance, Britain's Press Complaints Commission operates a code that gives reporters wide latitude to use subterfuge if the information sought is:
• In the public interest; and
• Not obtainable by open methods.
This permissive philosophy has produced many worthwhile investigative disclosures. One of the most ingenious came in the aftermath of Lockerbie [when Libyan terrorists destroyed a PanAm airliner in flight] when a newspaper and a TV station – separately – had staff obtain jobs as cleaners at London's Heathrow Airport. In that guise each was able to place a dummy bomb in parked jumbo jets – proving that security had not been made as foolproof as the authorities claimed.

When everybody else can have their say in print, there seems no reason why the government shouldn't too. But there is a far stronger case for a democratic government in a developing country to keep a presence in radio and television than in newspapers. This is partly because broadcasting has a vital development communication role, and it is uncertain that commercial interests would carry this out properly.

Also, alternative ownership models have their problems. The BBC model of non-commercial broadcasting is based on viewers' legal requirement to pay a licence fee. This means adequate arrangements to collect the fee, detect evaders and avoid corruption by those enforcing the system – a tall order in an advanced country and probably an impossible one here. The commercial model as in the main US networks raises extreme problems of low standards of programming as channels fall over themselves to win the ratings war as well as over-obtrusive advertising as channels chase the dollars.

ZANA could be sold to the Zambian news organisations, perhaps with some outside involvement, each organisation having an equity share in proportion to the capital provided. A socially more attractive solution, since it would tend to preserve jobs, is for the news organisations to be given Zana in exchange for a pledge to keep it going for a specified time.

It would take a stronger privatisation stomach than mine to accept the selling off of ZIS [Zambia Information Services]. Government information services continue to have a role all over the world. For developing countries they have a development communication function and also supply news from rural areas that the user media do not reach. Yet the winds of change have reached even here. British government departments do much of their own information and public relations work rather than putting it through the Central Office of Information (equivalent to a ministry of information). They are also free to contract out work so COI must sometimes compete for the job against private- companies.

So far, the liberalisation of the news media in Zambia has been encouraging if slow. The existence of the Weekly Post – vigorous, annoying and stimulating – is a fine advertisement for democracy here. Privatisation of media is being watched with interest in Africa and beyond. Because state control of information was never total (National Mirror etc.), so hopes now for an independent media are correspondingly higher.

PUBLICATION DATA

Barotseland and Scenes from Zambian Life
Published 2021 by
Edge Editions
Kings Nympton
Umberleigh EX37 9ST (UK)

www.ituri.co.uk

ISBN 9780992965877

Design by Rick Ives
Photo post-production by Ian Longthorne

COVER depicts sunset over the Zambezi, from an embroidered wall hanging by Pam Noel

continued overpage

PICTURE CREDITS

-Archive of the Northern Rhodesia Government, with acknowledgements (1)
-Cedric Pulford (2)
-Photograph of Lewanika, courtesy of Wikimedia Commons, shows the Litunga of Barotseland, during his visit to Edinburgh in 1902. The photo is credited to G.H. Tod. It is in the public domain in the United Kingdom, the United States and various other countries (3)
-Tony Noel (4)
-Tony Noel (5)
-*Northern News*, with acknowledgements (6)
-Tony Noel (7)
-Pam Noel (8)

Printed in the UK by 4Edge Ltd, on paper from sustainable sources
www.4edge.co.uk

Also in the Edge Editions minibook series:
A Horse Without a Carriage: Love and Marriage Through the Ages (2018) – Martin Horrocks